20 WAYS TO DRAW A DRESS

AND 23 OTHER FABULOUS FASHIONS AND ACCESSORIES

JULIA KUO

A Book for Artists, Designers, and Doodlers

Quarry Books
100 Cummings Center, Suite 406L
Beverly, MA 01915

quarrybooks.com • craftside.typepad.com

This library edition published in 2016 by Walter Foster Publishing,
a division of Quarto Publishing Group USA Inc.
6 Orchard Road, Suite 100
Lake Forest, CA 92630

© 2013 by Quarry Books
Illustrations © 2013 Julia Kuo
Text © 2013 Julia Kuo
First published in the United States of America in 2013 by
Quarry Books, a member of Quarto Publishing Group USA Inc.

Distributed in the United States and Canada by
Lerner Publisher Services
241 First Avenue North
Minneapolis, MN 55401 U.S.A.
www.lernerbooks.com

First Library Edition

Library of Congress Cataloging-in-Publication Data

Kuo, Julia.
   20 ways to draw a dress and 23 other fabulous fashions and accessories : a book for artists, designers, and doodlers / Julia Kuo. -- First library edition.
      pages cm
   ISBN 978-1-939581-73-0
   1. Fashion drawing. 2. Drawing--Technique. I. Title. II. Title: Book for artists, designers, and doodlers. III. Title: Twenty ways to draw a dress and twenty-three other fabulous fashions and accessories.
   TT509.K866 2016
   741.6'72--dc23

                                                                    2015002427

012016
1780

9 8 7 6 5 4 3 2 1

CONTENTS

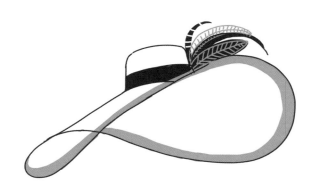

INTRODUCTION

LET'S LEARN HOW TO DRAW
clothes and accessories together! We pick outfits every
day based on where we're going, who we're meeting,
what the weather's like, and how we want to look. As a
form of self expression, fashion gives people around us
a little peek into what we're all about. It can say that
we're classy, unique, modern, laid-back, sporty, or a mixture of a few things. The
world of fashion is also constantly changing, giving us new collections and trends
every season to pick and choose from.

In this book, we've picked twenty-four different types of clothing and
accessories ranging from flats to ponchos to cocktail dresses. We've even got a few
items for guys. We've come up with twenty different ways that each of these items
can be drawn—can you come up with some of your own?

You can start out by trying to copy some of the items I've already drawn. Pick
your favorite on each page or combine different items to make an outfit that you
would wear. You can even pretend that you are a fashion editor or personal shopper
and pick out a collection of different items that you want to group together.

HOW TO USE THIS BOOK
These drawings are all made up of a combination of lines, shapes, and patterns.
Many fashion items are inspired by basic shapes, so look for squares, circles, and
triangles to help break down each object. Then consider the edges—should you
use a straight line, curved line, or a squiggly one? Draw the big shapes and lines
first, and then add in the smaller details. If you have tracing paper, you can trace

the drawings directly, but don't worry about getting them exactly the same.

When you think you've gotten the hang of it, try drawing your own fashion items and accessories. Think about what you've got in your own closet or that new bag you've got your eye on. Or be a fashion designer and come up with your own styles. How many ways can you draw a little black dress or a light, fall coat? What would your own summer collection of sandals and heels look like?

Try to start out with a pencil and eraser so that you're not afraid of making mistakes. When you feel more comfortable with drawing, explore by using different types of tools—pens, colored pencils, markers, or even paints. It's always fun to try as many things as possible to decide what you like the best.

Don't forget to show your friends and family when you're done. Maybe you'll inspire them to make their own drawings of their favorite fashions!

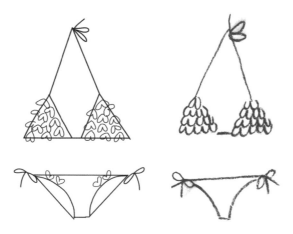

fur-top shoe: marker
dress: watercolor
bikini: colored pencil

DRAW 20
Cocktail Dresses

T-shirts

Men's Coats

HIGH HEELS

DRAW 20
SUNGLASSES

DRAW 20
Fur Coats

DRAW 20
Handbags

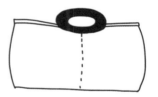

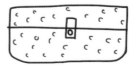

little black dresses

DRAW 20
TROUSERS

DRAW 20
Men's Hats

Blouses

DRAW 20
Swimsuits

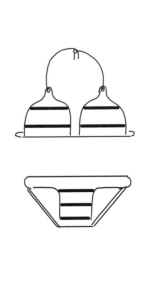

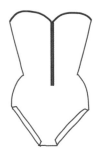

Animal Prints

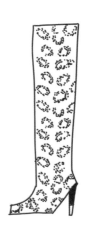

Skirts

DRAW 20
FLATS

DRAW 20
scarves

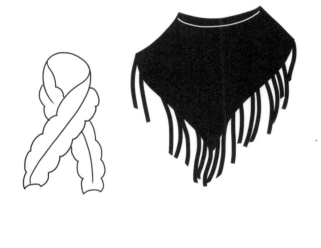

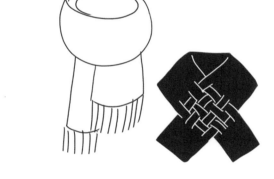

DRAW 20
Hats

Ties

TUNICS

DRAW 20
Sweaters

Men's Attire

Work Dresses

BELTS

DRAW 20
shorts

ABOUT THE ARTIST

Julia Kuo grew up in Los Angeles and studied illustration and marketing
at Washington University in St. Louis. She currently works as a freelance
illustrator in Chicago. Julia designs stationery, illustrates children's books,
concert posters, and CD covers and paints in her free time. One of her gallery
shows featured paintings of street fashion shots from Face Hunter. Julia's
clients include American Greetings, the *New York Times*, Little, Brown and
Company, Simon and Schuster, Capitol Records, and Universal Music Group.
She is also part of The Nimbus Factory, a collective of two designers and two
illustrators specializing in paper goods. Her illustrations have been honored in
American Illustration, CMYK magazine, and *Creative Quarterly*. **juliakuo.com**